The purejoojoo
Guide to Life

Thank you for being YOU

especially for YOU!

The purejoojoo Guide to Life

Change Your Life by Changing Your Thoughts

Isabel Mar

iUniverse, Inc.
Bloomington

The Purejoojoo Guide to Life
Change Your Life by Changing Your Thoughts

Copyright © 2011 by Isabel Mar.

All rights reserved. No part of this book may be used or reproduced by any means, graphic, electronic, or mechanical, including photocopying, recording, taping or by any information storage retrieval system without the written permission of the publisher except in the case of brief quotations embodied in critical articles and reviews.

iUniverse books may be ordered through booksellers or by contacting:

iUniverse
1663 Liberty Drive
Bloomington, IN 47403
www.iuniverse.com
1-800-Authors (1-800-288-4677)

Because of the dynamic nature of the Internet, any web addresses or links contained in this book may have changed since publication and may no longer be valid. The views expressed in this work are solely those of the author and do not necessarily reflect the views of the publisher, and the publisher hereby disclaims any responsibility for them.

Any people depicted in stock imagery provided by Thinkstock are models, and such images are being used for illustrative purposes only.
Certain stock imagery © Thinkstock.

ISBN: 978-1-4620-6662-9 (sc)
ISBN: 978-1-4620-6793-0 (ebk)

Library of Congress Control Number: 2011960846

Purejoojoo logo designed
by Gonzalo Rodríguez
www. logonberry.com

Printed in the United States of America

iUniverse rev. date: 12/08/2011

INTRODUCTION

If you want to make a change in your life, then *The Purejoojoo Guide to Life* is for you.

If you want to live up to your potential, then *The Purejoojoo Guide to Life* is for you.

If you want to get out of your rut, then *The Purejoojoo Guide to Life* is for you.

If you want to start living your life, then *The Purejoojoo Guide to Life* is for you.

The only thing standing in your way is *you*.

Your own thoughts are preventing you from living the life that you want.

Your own thoughts are stopping you from being everything you know you can be.

Your own thoughts are sabotaging your confidence and belief in yourself.

Your own thoughts are holding you back.

That's why you are suffering.

When you are unaware of your own thoughts, you begin to lose your sense of self because you start to think that you need to do it all and be everything to everyone.

When you are unaware of your own thoughts, you begin to lose your sense of control because you start to think that you need to live at the same pace as everyone else and there is no time to just be still.

When you are unaware of your thoughts, you begin to lose your sense of worth because you start to think that your worth is outside of yourself and tied to the size of your body, the size of your house, the size of your paycheck.

When you are unaware of your thoughts, you begin to lose your sense of purpose because you start to think unconsciously and allow other people's thoughts to determine how you should be, how you should look, how you should live.

Take back control of your life by taking back control of your thoughts.

Become aware of your thoughts by consciously thinking good thoughts and replacing negative ones with positive ones.

Become aware of your thoughts by coming back to your breath and taking time to be still.

Become aware of your thoughts by returning to your own love, where no suffering can exist.

The only things you can control in life are

- your thoughts,
- your breath,
- and your love.

Once you realize this, then you can start to learn how to make positive changes in your life, for good.

The Purejoojoo Guide to Life will show you how to change your life by changing your thoughts.

The Purejoojoo Guide to Life will show you how to return to your breath.

The Purejoojoo Guide to Life will show you how to arrive back at your own love.

It all starts with one thought: the decision to begin.

One thought can begin to change your life for good.

One single thought.

The book you are holding in your hands is the result of that one single thought.

Change your life by changing your thoughts.

It is possible.

The Choice

Are you ready for a change?

Are you tired of feeling unhappy?

Have you had enough?

You can make a change.

Do you feel lost?

Do you feel like you have no direction or purpose?

Have you lost your sense of self?

The only thing you need to find is your own love.

Are you stuck?

Are you bored?

Do you feel like life is passing you by?

All you need to do is begin to be aware.

Does the world seem like a bad place?

Does life feel hopeless?

Do you feel hopeless?

Change Your Life by Changing Your Thoughts

You are deserving of love.

Have you given up on yourself?

Have you given up on life?

Are your thoughts filled with negativity?

Choose to think positively.

Do you feel all alone?

Are you simply existing?

Do all your days feel the same?

Come alive through your breath.

When was the last time you felt alive?

When was the last time you felt love?

When was the last time you smiled?

Reconnect with your own love first.

Do you feel like you matter?

You do.

This is your life.

Every day, your life is getting shorter, whether you decide to live it or not.

Every day, you have a choice to live your life or not.

Every day, you can make positive changes for good.

You are worth the effort.

You matter.

You can do this.

You can change your life right now.

You can change your life in this moment.

All you need to do is choose to begin.

Change Your Life by Changing Your Thoughts.

Creating positive change in your life begins with one thought: the commitment to the daily practice of replacing negative, self-destructive thoughts with positive, healthy ones.

This one fundamental change will change your thoughts for good.

This one fundamental change will change your life for good.

This one fundamental change will change *you* for good.

Choose to start making positive changes in your life for good.

Choose to start committing to you . . . and your own success . . . and your own joy.

Choose to start living your life.

Change your life by changing your thoughts.

Are you ready?

Life Just Is.

Life just is.

Think about this.

The only difference between someone who sees life as good and someone who sees life as bad is their thoughts.

Life isn't doing anything to anyone. Life isn't selective. Life doesn't play favorites. Life doesn't choose.

You choose how to think or not think about life.

You choose how to live or not live your life.

You choose how to feel or not feel every day of your life.

Until you accept that life just is, until you realize that there is no such thing as good or bad, until you see that life isn't doing anything to you and it is up to you to choose to live your life or let it pass you by, there will always be a constant battle within yourself, because you are trying to control something that is beyond your control.

You control your thoughts.

You are the only one who decides what thoughts are allowed to enter your mind and what thoughts are denied entry.

You are the only one who decides what thoughts to let go and what thoughts will stay.

You are the only one who decides every day which thoughts to focus on—over and over and over again.

And it is only *you* who can choose to change your thoughts for good.

You can choose to create a life of pure joy and contentment or to create a life of despair and sadness.

You can choose to be happy every day or be miserable.

You can choose to love yourself or not to.

Your thoughts create your reality.

Your thoughts have created the life that you have right now.

Your thoughts can create the life that you have always imagined.

Change your life by changing your thoughts.

What are you waiting for?

Choose to Think Positive.

Take a moment to think about the thoughts you have about your body. Do you like your body? Do you appreciate your body? Do you respect your body? Or do you hate your body? Do you punish your body? Do you fight against your body?

What about your job? Do you like your job? Do you appreciate your job? Do you respect your job? Or do you hate waking up every morning to go to work? Do you count the days until the weekend? Do you wish you were doing something else?

Now think about yourself. Do you like yourself? Do you appreciate yourself? Do you respect yourself? Do you feel good about yourself? Do you feel love for yourself? Do you feel like you are making a difference? Do you enjoy life? Do you feel joy? Do you feel love? Do you feel *alive*?

If you have negative thoughts about your body or your job or yourself, why is this?

It's because your thoughts continue to be about how unhappy you are, how miserable you are, how unfair life is, how hard life is, how no one understands, how no one cares, how hopeless things are, how nothing ever changes.

And you repeat these thoughts over and over and over again in your head until your reality, your life becomes exactly what your thoughts made it—and worse, you begin to believe that this is who you are and what life is.

And you keep practicing them over and over and over in your head until you don't even have to think about it anymore because it has become instinctive to think this way as your natural response to whatever happens to you in life.

All your thoughts have become unconscious—just because everyone else is doing it.

You have become unaware of your thoughts and simply allow the negative, self-destructive thoughts to persist in your head.

You have given control of your thoughts to someone else instead of thinking for yourself.

Now think about becoming fully conscious and aware of your thoughts.

Instead of focusing on negative, self-destructive thoughts like, *I am not good enough*, *I hate myself*, *No one loves me*, *I am not worthy of love*, what if you started thinking positive, healthy thoughts like, *I am good enough! I am loved! I am love! I love who I am!*

What if you started to consciously think about these thoughts over and over and over again in your head until you started to believe these thoughts instead of the negative, self-destructive ones?

What if you started to live these new, positive, healthy thoughts every single day of your life?

What if you started to be these new, positive thoughts?

The only difference between negative thoughts and positive ones is *you*.

You choose what thoughts to think about every single day.

You choose what thoughts shape your reality of yourself, of others, and of life.

You choose what thoughts you will believe about yourself, about others, and about life.

So why not choose to love yourself?

Why not choose to love others?

Why not choose to love life?

Our thoughts create our reality.

Change your life by changing your thoughts.

Think about it.

Begin with just being aware of the thoughts that come up in your head.

Begin with just being aware of your thoughts so you can slowly start the process of replacing negative thoughts with positive ones.

It is possible.

Choose to live your life.

Choose to create your life.

Choose to love your life.

Choose to love yourself.

It is your choice.

What will you choose to do?

The Process of Positive Change.

Now that you have decided to begin the process of positive change, you must first understand that it is a lifelong process.

Do not feel daunted by this. Do not be afraid.

Once you understand what a *process* is, you will begin to not only appreciate it but you will start seeing the beauty in it and will simply be amazed.

Begin the process of choosing to think positively every day.

And the more you practice it again and again and again, the better you will get at it!

Think about it.

Make it a daily practice to learn how to be happy, to learn how to live fully, to learn how to love completely.

You only get better at those things which you practice, so with each precious day, you can learn to be happier, learn to live more fully, learn to love more completely!

And this process can continue for the rest of your life.

Think about that!

Choose to think positively—again and again and again.

Change your life by changing your thoughts.

Think about it.

So what is a *process*?

A process is a series of steps that produce a result.

So if you want to create positive changes in your life, understand first that it is a process where a sequence of steps needs to occur in a certain order.

And if you try to control the order of the steps, you will simply end up producing feelings of frustration and defeat.

Just like a bud needs time to blossom, a heart needs time to learn compassion and forgiveness.

Just like bread needs time to rise, a mind needs time to unlearn negative thinking and relearn positive thinking.

What does the process of positive thinking look like?

It looks like this:

- You will continue to have the negative thoughts because they are now part of your reality.
- But just like you allowed these thoughts to enter your mind, you can also allow new, positive thoughts to enter your mind—and this time, you will be fully conscious and aware of them.
- When a negative thought arrives—and it will—you will consciously replace it with a positive one.
- And you will keep doing this over and over and over again.
- Some days, you will do better than others, and some days, you will fall back into your old thought patterns of negativity and nonlove; but the difference will be that you are now aware that you are doing it.

- The more aware you are, the more you will refuse to allow these negative thoughts to continue.
- You will choose to replace them with positive thoughts until the positive thoughts begin to outweigh the negative ones.
- And then the positive thoughts will become your natural response to life!

It is possible.

It is going to take time and daily practice and effort, because any thought in your head will always be there.

However, you can control how often that thought comes back and the intensity of that thought.

Daily Effort.

Think of thoughts as seeds.

It is up to you which thoughts you choose to water so they can grow.

If you choose to water the negative ones, then you will have a garden of self-destructive and unforgiving thoughts in your head, which will continue to spread to your outlook on life, your opinion of others, and your view of yourself.

But if you choose to water only positive ones, then you will have a garden of healthy and happy thoughts in your head, which will continue to spread to your outlook on life, your opinion of others, and your view of yourself.

You just need to practice again and again and again.

You just need to make the daily effort again and again and again.

You are already making the daily effort to think negatively. You are just not aware of it, and you do it now unconsciously because you have gotten so good at it.

So why not choose to make the daily effort to think positively and get so good at that?

Change your life by changing your thoughts.

What are you waiting for?

Give yourself time to allow the positive change to happen by understanding what a process is.

Then learn to accept and appreciate the process—the process of positive change, the process of thinking positive ... the process of coming alive.

The Wholeness of Life.

Respect for the process is the one requirement to create positive changes for good.

So if you want to change your life for good, then you must respect the process of change.

Respect for the process means total understanding and acceptance of the wholeness of life.

What does *wholeness* mean?

It means day and night.

It means joy and sorrow.

It means love and pain.

It means life and death.

Accepting the wholeness of life means letting go of control.

Accepting the wholeness of life means letting go of the thought that you can control anything other than your own thoughts.

Accept that there is suffering in the world but also joy and happiness.

Accept that we are all going to die, so choose to live every day.

Accept that we are human and imperfect and we have the ability to think, so there will always be struggle. Why not learn to forgive, accept, and love ourselves and each other since we are all going through this experience called life together?

Accept the wholeness of life and understand that you have a choice of what to focus your thoughts on, every moment of every day.

It Is Never Too Late.

You can always make positive changes in your life.

It is never too late.

End the struggle to try to control things that can't be controlled.

End the willfullness to try to control how life will unfold.

End the effort to try to be someone other than who you are right now.

It is possible.

Change your life by changing your thoughts.

What are you waiting for?

Be the One.

The process of any change is not easy, and the process of positive change has an added level of difficulty because it is not the norm.

Most people choose to be miserable because it is easier to be unhappy than it is to make the effort to be happy.

Most people choose to let life pass them by because it takes less effort than creating a life.

Most people choose to simply exist because it has become an unconscious state of mind that no longer requires any thought.

Do you realize how crazy that is? People are allowing themselves to be miserable and unhappy and depressed and feel worthless and inadequate and unloved—just because everyone else is doing it?

Be the one to change your thoughts for good.

Be the one to change your life for good.

Be the one to inspire others to do the same.

Change your life by changing your thoughts.

Are you ready?

Experience It for Yourself.

You will only begin to understand what the process of positive change is when you experience it for yourself.

It can only happen if you decide to let yourself go through it, let yourself experience it, let yourself feel it fully and completely.

Until you try it, you will never know what it feels like, what it looks like, what it tastes like.

Until you do it, you will never know what it means to appreciate the beauty in the struggle.

Until you do it, you will never know what it means to be truly alive.

You have nothing to lose other than all the negative, self-destructive, self-loathing, and self-punishing thoughts that have been holding you back.

You have nothing to lose other than another day of not living your life.

Change your life by changing your thoughts.

Let the process of positive change begin!

Return to the Breath.

Now that you have an understanding of what a process is, you can now start the process of positive change by choosing to think positive.

And it all begins with the breath.

One single breath.

Just like we all started our lives with one single breath, the process of positive change begins with a single breath and the daily practice of returning to the breath.

When you breathe, you are perfectly in the moment.

You are completely aware of the moment—not the one that has passed, not the one that will be coming next, but this very moment.

By being completely aware, you are fully conscious of what it is you are doing, and you will realize that there is no mind in this conscious moment when you are one with the breath. There are no thoughts running through your head, no worries to weigh you down, nobody to be distracted by.

There is only you and your breath, you and your awareness, you and your conscious thought.

And this is how positive change begins.

Become aware of your thoughts in order to start changing your life.

It begins with letting go of all your thoughts with one single breath.

Take a moment and just sit.

Close your eyes and just inhale through your nose with your mouth closed, filling your belly with your breath so it expands like a big balloon. Hold it for a moment.

Then slowly release the breath through your nose and from your belly. Just take a moment to experience this calm ... this grace ... this moment.

Now think about something that makes you feel good.

Just live in this moment for a while.

Allow yourself to fully experience the remembered experience and how it made you feel and how it makes you feel right now.

Then release the thought and simply be still.

Simply be present.

Simply be.

Notice how relaxed you are.

Observe how calm your breath is.

Recognize how still your mind is.

Realize that you are one in the moment.

You have just experienced positive change.

You have taught yourself with one simple thought how to be present again, how to be aware again, how to be alive again.

You returned to the breath and became one again with the moment.

You felt it.

You experienced it.

You lived it.

Learning to Be Aware.

Now it is just a matter of repeating this feeling over and over and over again until calmness and contentment, happiness and quiet joy become your natural response, your natural state, instead of worry and anxiety, misery and shame.

Be aware of your thoughts.

Be mindful of the thoughts that you allow yourself to think.

Be conscious and present in your daily life so you begin to start changing the way you respond to life, respond to situations, respond to people.

Experience it for yourself.

It is the only way to become fully alive and to create positive changes for good.

It is the only way.

This is what it means to be fully aware, fully conscious ... this is what it means to be fully alive.

Experience life by returning to the breath of life—again and again and again.

Your breath is available to you anywhere, anytime.

Keep returning to your breath and keep returning to life.

Keep returning to love.

Keep returning to your own love.

Whenever life becomes overwhelming, simply remember to return to the breath wherever you are, and you will find the oneness of the moment, the oneness within yourself, the oneness of love ... the oneness where we are all connected as human beings.

Returning to the breath is a learned behavior.

If you have never been conscious of your breath, this is also a learned behavior, a learned response that has simply been practiced over and over and over again.

But like anything learned, it can be unlearned with daily practice and effort.

So if you are ready to start making positive changes for good in your life, begin to practice returning to the breath again and again and again until you become so good at it that *this* becomes your natural response to life!

The Gift of Your Life.

Similar to your breath, which is constantly flowing, life is constantly flowing, and it is up to you how you will choose to ride the wave of life every single day.

If this is a daunting prospect, then you simply have not realized that you have been given a gift—the most precious gift in the world. It is called your life.

You have been given this privilege of being alive, this gift of being born, this present of being here, right now.

You can choose to live it or you can choose to simply let it pass you by.

It is up to you.

You have the choice every single day to create the masterpiece that you know your life can be; it all begins with your thoughts.

It is your choice to live or to simply exist.

Choose to live your life.

Choose to create your life.

Choose to create positive changes in your life for good, because you are good, people are good, and life is already good.

What will you choose?

Your Thoughts Create Your Reality.

If you are ready to truly live, then begin with your thoughts.

If you are ready to truly come alive, then begin with your thoughts.

If you are ready to experience what it means to have your heart sing, your mind released, and your body flow, then begin with your thoughts.

When you begin with your thoughts, you will begin to understand what it means to be *so* in love with life and *so* in love with love, because you are *so* in love with yourself.

Your thoughts create your reality.

Your views about life, about people, are 100 percent tied to the thoughts that you have about yourself.

If you hate any part of yourself, then you will find it easy to hate parts of life, hate parts of other people.

If you are judging yourself against unrealistic standards and being overly critical, then you will undoubtedly be quick to judge another with this same criticalness and harsh standard.

You will be less accepting of others because you do not accept yourself unconditionally.

You will be less forgiving of others because you do not forgive yourself unconditionally.

You will be less loving of others because you do not love yourself unconditionally.

If you are punishing yourself for not being good enough, for falling short of some ideal set by someone else, for not being "perfect," then you will certainly be punishing another for the same reasons.

Once you realize that your life is what your thoughts make it, then you can truly begin to create positive changes in your life for good.

You choose every thought that you allow to enter into your head.

You also choose every thought that you refuse to allow into your head.

Never give this choice away to anyone else.

Don't allow someone else to create your life.

Don't let society dictate what you should be, how you should look, when you should accomplish things.

Don't let others mandate what your life should look like and how you should live.

Take back control of your life by taking back control of your thoughts.

This means that you need to practice being aware and conscious of your thoughts.

This means that you need to accept full responsibility of your life right now.

This means that you are about to create the life that you have always imagined.

Make the effort every day, because you are worth it.

Make the effort every day, because life is worth it.

Make the effort every day, because *your* life is worth it.

Full Responsibility for Your Life.

If you truly want to create positive changes in your life for good, if you truly want to take control of your life, if you truly want to live your life, you need to accept full responsibility for all the thoughts that you have about yourself, about others and about life right now.

You need to accept that you are the only one who has created the reality you are living right now.

So if you are unhappy, you created this.

You need to accept the choices you have made in your life that have created the reality you are living right now.

So if you are miserable, you created this.

But by the same token, you also have the power to create something different.

You have the power to change your life right now.

You have the power to recreate your life into everything you always wanted it to be.

And you have already begun.

Continue the process by starting to let go of the blame.

Continue the process by starting to let go of the shame.

Continue the process by starting to just let go of it all.

Let go of the negative thoughts.

Let go of the self-punishment.

Let go of the perfection.

Let go of the judgment.

Let go of the notion that the world revolves around you.

Because once you realize that it is not all about you, you can begin to release yourself completely from the vicious cycle of negative thinking and begin a new cycle of positive thinking!

Think about it.

Just like all your thoughts are focused on why you are the only one feeling unhappy, that is exactly how other people are thinking too.

Just like all your thoughts are focused on why you are the only one being inconvenienced, that is exactly how other people are thinking too.

Just like all your thoughts are focused on why you are the only one going through this, that is exactly what other people are thinking too.

You need to understand that they are not thinking about you!

They are only thinking of themselves just like you are only thinking about yourself.

So if everyone else is thinking about themselves, then why are you so worried about what other people think?

Why are you killing yourself to be an ideal that you think somebody else wants you to be?

Why are you obsessed with living a life that is not yours but somebody else's definition?

Once you realize this truth, you can begin to release yourself from the pressures, the expectations, the standards that were not even real to begin with.

They were all in your head!

And if you don't believe it, then try this.

Return to the moment by returning to your breath.

Close your eyes and begin to release all the negative thoughts from your mind and replace them with only positive thoughts.

Allow your mind to be filled with only positive thoughts about yourself, about others, about life.

When your mind is calm, begin to open your eyes. Give the biggest smile you've got to the next person you see.

Give someone the smile that radiates from the innermost core of your being where you are love, where you are safe, and where you are loved.

See what happens!

It is only through direct experience that you will know with complete certainty that joy and happiness, pure love, and complete bliss come from within.

It has nothing to do with your body.

It has nothing to do with your income level.

It has nothing to do with your marital status.

It has nothing to do with the size of your house, the make of your car, the label on your clothes, the title on your business card.

It has everything to do with you and your light and your love and your presence.

And you can shine your light right now.

You can share your love right now.

You can give the gift of your presence right now to someone else and remind them of how wonderful they already are. In doing so, you will be giving yourself the best gift in the world: the gift of *you*.

You are the only you in this world.

You are the only you in this life.

You are the only you who can choose to share yourself with the world.

And all you need to do is change your thoughts about *you*.

Think about it.

Change your life by changing your thoughts.

Return to Your Own Love.

Once you begin to return to your own love, your own acceptance, your own forgiveness, you can begin to love, accept, and forgive others, because you are now love, acceptance, and forgiveness.

You now see others in the same way because you now love, accept, and forgive yourself.

You now see life in the same way because you now love, accept, and forgive yourself.

The way to return to love, to acceptance, to forgiveness is to think of the other person.

The way back to love is to remember that the other person is also suffering.

The way back to acceptance is to remember that we are all the same.

The way back to forgiveness is to remember that we are human.

Be the one to show compassion first.

Be the one to love first.

Be the one to create positive change.

Be for love and you will find love ... you will find your own love again.

Return to your own love by helping others to do the same.

Think about it.

Change your life by changing your thoughts—and change other people's lives too.

Dissolve into the Process.

So you may be thinking, *How realistic is it to be aware of every thought? How is it possible to control every thought?*

It's not.

And it is not necessary.

Because it is a process.

A process is a continuous flow.

Just like life.

Life just is.

There is no expectation.

There is no force.

So all you need to do is begin, and keep practicing and making the daily effort again and again and again.

Lose all preconceived notions of what it is supposed to look like, all expectations of what it is supposed to feel like, all judgment of what it is supposed to be.

Simply let go and allow yourself to experience it.

Simply let go and allow yourself to feel it.

Simply let go and allow yourself to see it.

Simply let go and allow yourself to be it.

Eventually, you will simply dissolve into the process and flow with life.

All you need to do is start replacing one negative thought at a time.

There is no timeline.

There is no pressure.

It is a constant flow of learning and unlearning.

It is a process of acceptance and forgiveness.

Make the effort every day and *be amazed*!

The negative thoughts will always be part of your thought process and can resurface at any time, but through the daily practice of replacing negative thoughts with positive ones, you will build your confidence in your ability to focus on positive thoughts first. Any fear of the old negative way of thinking disappears because positive thinking will prevail.

So even though the negative thoughts will always exist, you just need to recognize that the thought has arrived.

Be aware of it.

Don't fight it.

Simply take a moment to recognize its presence, and for the first time in your life, consciously say, "No!" to the thought, either in your mind or out loud.

That one act of saying, "No!"—that one conscious thought of refusing to accept the negative thought in your head—begins the process of positive change for good.

So the next time the same self-destructive thought arrives (and it will!), you consciously say, "No!" again either in your mind or out loud, and begin replacing the negative thought with a positive one, until eventually, the new positive thought arrives instead of the old negative one.

It takes practice.

It takes effort.

It takes time.

It takes awareness.

It takes conscious thought.

And it takes love.

But it *will* happen.

And the more you practice replacing negative thoughts with positive ones, the more you will begin to respond differently to the same situations that used to set you off or annoy you and just drive you crazy.

Why?

Because you are returning to your own acceptance.

Because you are returning to your own forgiveness.

Because you are returning to your own love.

And when you forgive yourself, when you accept yourself, when you love yourself again, everything changes.

Everything changes for good.

You begin to see things differently because you are now thinking of things differently.

You find yourself in the same body, in the same job, in the same relationship, but everything looks slightly different—fresh, new.

Everything seems lighter.

Everything looks brighter.

Everything feels better.

And the *only* thing that has changed is your thoughts: your thoughts about life, your thoughts about others, and most of all, your thoughts about yourself.

Positive Thinking.

Let's look at the questions at the start of this book to allow you to experience some positive thoughts that you may not have considered.

Are you ready for a change?

Life is constantly changing. You are constantly changing. Your body is constantly changing. Change is good.

Are you tired of feeling unhappy?

The fact that you can still feel anything means you are still alive. Use your unhappiness as a beautiful reminder that you are ready to make a positive change in your life.

Have you had enough?

Again, this is a good feeling to have because it means that you are done with these feelings and ready to experience new ones. Embrace the frustration, the anger, the despair, and realize that all these feelings are opportunities for positive change to heal, to forgive … to love.

Do you feel lost?

There is nothing to be found except your own love.

Do you feel like you have no direction or purpose?

Find your way back to your own love and you will know your purpose.

Have you lost your sense of self?

Take moments for yourself every day, unapologetically, in order to keep giving of yourself to others and to life.

Are you stuck?

Stop doing and be still. Experience the beauty in the silence, in the stillness.

Are you bored?

Stop thinking and be still. Experience the beauty in the silence, in the stillness.

Do you feel like life is passing you by?

Start living and feel alive. Notice life around you and start participating. You are welcome to join in. Everyone is welcome. No invitation required. Come as you are.

Does the world seem like a bad place?

The world is a beautiful place. It is simply our thoughts that make us think that it is something other than absolutely beautiful. Our thoughts form the world. Make your contribution to make the world even more beautiful.

Does life feel hopeless?

Life just is, which means you have the choice every day to create something beautiful.

Do you feel hopeless?

There is always hope. You are already good. You are already enough.

Have you given up on yourself?

Never give up ... on you, on life, on others. Simply give in to the feelings that you are experiencing right now and learn to get out of your head so you can get up and feel alive again.

Have you given up on life?

Life will never give up on you. All you need to do is notice all the life around you waiting for you to let it in.

Are your thoughts filled with negativity?

Choose to think positively only. All your negative thoughts were learned. So you can unlearn them and learn to have only positive thoughts. It is possible.

Do you feel all alone?

We are all connected. Ask for help and see what happens. We have all been there.

Are you simply existing?

Exist for something and then you will truly start to live.

Do all your days feel the same?

Find the magical in the mundane. Find the wonder in the worry. Find the beauty in the struggle.

When was the last time you felt alive?

Begin with yourself and realize that you are here right now. You are alive. You have breath. You have everything you need to change your life simply by changing one thought to this: *I am love.*

When was the last time you felt love?

Begin with yourself and feel your own love. You can always feel love by returning to your own love, your own forgiveness, your own acceptance. You have all the love you need simply by changing one thought to this: *I am love.*

When was the last time you truly smiled?

Begin with yourself and experience your own smile. Smile because you are already who you need to be. Smile because you are already where you need to be. Smile because you can. Smile because you are slowly beginning to change your thoughts to *I am love.*

DO YOU FEEL LIKE YOU MATTER?

Yes! Yes! Yes!

It is your choice.

What will you choose to do?

Just Try.

Choose to commit to your own acceptance.

Choose to commit to your own forgiveness.

Choose to commit to your own love.

You will never know until you try.

So why not give it a chance?

Change your life by changing your thoughts.

Our thoughts are forming the world.

Think about it.

A Direct Reflection.

Once your return to your own love, return to your own acceptance, return to your own forgiveness, then you can begin to think about others and life in the same way.

You begin to react with calmness and compassion because you are now coming from a place of acceptance.

You respond with less judgment and criticism because you are now coming from a place of forgiveness.

You are open to receiving all of what life has to offer—all of its possibilities and opportunities, gifts and joys—because you are now coming from a place of pure love and joy!

Your life is a direct reflection of your thoughts.

Why not think positive thoughts about others?

Why not think positive thoughts about life?

Why not think *only* positive thoughts about yourself?

Think about it.

Change your life by changing your thoughts.

The Beauty in the Struggle.

Keep reminding yourself that learning to replace negative thoughts with positive ones is a process.

It will not happen instantly and it will not happen without daily practice and effort.

So if you continue to learn to accept the undeniable fact that positive change is a lifelong process and continue to practice accepting the wholeness of life, then you can begin to appreciate the beauty in the struggle.

Once you do, then even the struggle is no longer thought of as a struggle; you begin to think of it as an opportunity to grow, a lesson to continue to learn, and yet another gift that life has bestowed upon you!

So now that you understand that any positive change is a process and it is your choice every single day to choose to make the effort to replace negative thoughts with positive ones, how do you stay motivated?

How do you stay focused?

How do you stay committed to creating positive change for good?

Purejoojoo positive energy!

Purejoojoo Positive Energy.

Purejoojoo is pure positive energy.

We all have it.

We all feel it.

It is our choice every single day to share it with others and the world or to simply let it remain unused and unlit inside of us.

It is the light that each one of us has within ourselves to shine to others and radiate to the world.

It is the love that each one of us has to bestow upon ourselves and to others.

Purejoojoo is what you feel when you give something of yourself to others.

Purejoojoo is what you get in return when someone gives something of themselves to you.

Purejoojoo is the pure positive energy that surrounds us all at all times if we allow ourselves to be open to receiving it.

Purejoojoo is the energy that you have when you are filled with love, filled with life, filled with light.

Purejoojoo is what you feel when you are truly alive and completely aware of the moment, when you are living with conscious thought and totally connected to everyone and everything around you.

Purejoojoo is when you allow yourself to let go and let love in.

Purejoojoo is what you feel when you return to the breath, return to the oneness of the moment, the oneness of love, the oneness where we are all connected, the oneness where we are all experiencing this gift of life together.

Purejoojoo is when you are absolutely present in the moment ... right here, right now.

You are purejoojoo positive energy!

All you need to do is be aware of your brilliance, your beauty, your light *right now*.

Then choose to radiate it to the world and to everyone you meet.

Choose to focus on positive thoughts instead of negative ones.

Choose to focus on spreading pure, positive energy instead of negative energy.

Choose to focus on love instead of nonlove.

It all begins with *you* ... and one choice to change your thoughts for good.

We can all do it if we so choose.

We can all give it if we so choose.

We can all receive it if we so choose.

We can all live our lives with pure joy and contentment if we choose to make the effort and practice every day.

What will you choose?

Think about it.

Change your life by changing your thoughts.

Reconnect.

We are all connected, and if you don't believe this, then it is only because you have lost your connection with your own acceptance, your own forgiveness ... your own love.

You have become so caught up with *you* that you have forgotten about anyone and anything else.

You have isolated yourself from receiving all the love that is around you right now.

Reconnect with others.

Reconnect with life.

Reconnect with yourself.

Reconnect with your humanness.

Being Human.

We are all experiencing this thing called life together.

We are all going through this thing called life together.

We are all dealing with the same struggles in this thing called life together.

We are all human.

Being human means being imperfect, being lonely, being sad, being frustrated, being rejected, being embarrassed, being lost.

And being human also means being happy, being joyful, being silly, being in love, being filled with love.

By returning to our humanness and allowing ourselves to be imperfect, we release ourselves so we can begin the process of positive change for good.

By returning to our humanness and allowing ourselves to be imperfect, we can heal ourselves so we can begin the process of positive change for good.

By returning to our humanness and allowing ourselves to be imperfect, we can find our own love again, which is where all positive change for good begins.

When you return to your own acceptance, when you return to your own forgiveness, when you return to your own love, you become filled with an energy that cannot be contained.

The energy must be shared with others and with the world.

The energy becomes transformed into a pure joy of life that simply must be released.

And this energy is purejoojoo!

The only thing that you need to do is be *100 percent you!*

Radiate Your Purejoojoo.

You will simply radiate positive energy from your entire being—your eyes, your touch, your actions, your words, your thoughts, your smile.

This is your purejoojoo positive energy to share with others and with the world, if you so choose.

If you do choose to share your purejoojoo positive energy with others and with the world, then you will also receive purejoojoo positive energy from others and from the world!

It is a continuous cycle that will never end, and it will allow you to continue to return to pure love, to total acceptance, to unconditional forgiveness for good.

But you need to make the conscious choice every day to give and to receive.

You need to be aware that this is a daily choice to give and to receive.

Experience it for yourself.

It is the *only* way to begin to create positive changes for good in your life.

Do it.

Feel it.

See it.

Be it.

So the next person you see, radiate your purejoojoo positive energy with a smile or a kind word or a gesture of kindness.

Give yourself to the other person by being completely present and aware of the moment that you are both sharing.

Experience it for yourself and *be amazed*.

Think about it.

Change your life by changing your thoughts.

The Destination Is Your Own Love.

Now you are beginning to realize that your very presence is a gift to others, a gift to the world.

When you return to love again and again and again, you allow yourself to be open to life, open to others, open to love.

When you return to love again and again and again, you are able to give your best self to others and to the world.

When you return to love again and again and again, you practice acceptance, forgiveness, and purelove for not only yourself but for others and for the world.

In doing so, you allow others to return to love so that they too can start spreading their purejoojoo positive energy!

Keep returning to acceptance.

Keep returning to forgiveness.

Keep returning to love.

Keep returning to your own acceptance.

Keep returning to your own forgiveness.

Keep returning to your own love.

It is your natural state.

It is possible.

It begins with *you*.

You can return to love in this moment.

You can return to love right now.

Simply choose to let go of the negativity for this moment.

Choose to let go of the self-hate and the self-loathing for this moment.

Choose to love yourself for this moment fully, completely, and unconditionally.

Choose to return to the breath and just be here in this moment.

Experience this one moment when you are simply filled with love only.

Experience this one moment when you are one with your breath, one with the moment, one with life.

Just savor it.

Be in it.

Live it.

Breathe it.

Be it.

Then it is just a matter of practice to keep returning to this place again and again and again where you are filled with love, where you are one with love, where you are connected to all the love that is around you and that is within you, waiting to come out.

You will begin to realize that what you have been searching for has been inside of you all this time.

The search for happiness, for success, for fulfillment—all you needed to do was return to your own acceptance, your own forgiveness, your own love.

Your destination is *you*.

Your destination is your own love.

Keep returning to your own love, and every time you arrive at this place, be thankful and appreciate it for as long as you can, because this is where pure joy exists and pure contentment lives.

And it has been patiently waiting for you to return, patiently waiting for your arrival ... for you to stay for good.

Think about it.

Take a moment and think about it.

Return to the breath and think about it.

The only thing that you need to find is your own love.

It has been inside of you all along, waiting for you to return to it.

Your own love is what you can control completely.

You can choose not to love yourself or you can choose to love yourself fully, completely, unconditionally.

And you get to *choose* every single day.

It all begins with your thoughts.

And if you decide to choose to love, your entire life will change for good.

All you need to do is decide and then make the commitment to practice every day, accept that it is a process, and be completely open to all the amazing opportunities that life will bring your way!

Begin with your thoughts.

Return to the breath.

Arrive back at your own love.

Accept yourself.

Forgive yourself.

Love yourself.

Then you will begin to accept others, forgive others, love others.

Begin to accept life, forgive life … love life.

It all begins with a single thought: a simple thought to love.

Always assume the best.

Always look at both sides.

Always remember that the other person is suffering.

Practice compassion—for yourself and for others.

Be for love rather than against it.

Be for you rather than against you.

Change Your Life by Changing Your Thoughts

You are love.

You are released.

You are here right now.

So long as you have breath, you can change your thoughts.

So long as you have breath, you can change your life.

Just breathe, and keep returning to the breath.

This you can do, right here, right now.

This you can do . . . for you.

This you can do . . . do it now.

Change your life by changing your thoughts.

What are you waiting for?

powered by purejoojoo.com

ABOUT THE AUTHOR

Isabel Mar enjoys the simple pleasures of life. She finds the magical in the mundane and the extraordinary in the ordinary. She has affected many with her contagious smile, her infectious energy and her positive outlook. She currently lives in Colorado.

CPSIA information can be obtained at www.ICGtesting.com
Printed in the USA
BVOW022108050112

279930BV00005B/41/P